JANINE OLIVIA

ENTERPRISES

You have the Power
to chase happiness!

Janine
"JJ"

Conway

1

2

Also by Janine "JJ" Conway
(formerly Janine Wiggins)

Focused, Effective, Fundraising
The Trustee Handbook
Overcome Inertia
Fix Your Money, Find Your Honey
Stop Blocking Your Legacy
The 7 Secrets of Abundance Attraction

40 Dates in 4 Months

My Crazy "Single Again" Online Dating Adventure

By Janine Conway

40 Dates in 4 Months by Janine Conway

First Printing: 2017

ISBN-13: 978-1985262157
ISBN-10: 1985262150

www.JJConway.org

The characters in this book are composites of many people with names and details changed to protect their identities.

Thanks to:

God the Father
My Lord and Savior
The Precious Holy Spirit
And, of course, my loving family!

This book is dedicated to the members of
the singles groups I founded:

Kingstowne Christian Singles
(now under the leadership of Dave and Patty Wheeler)

Shreveport-Bossier Christian Singles
(which I continue to run)

Table of Contents

Introduction

Why so many dates in such a short period of time?

I wish I could say I had an inspiring, world-changing, higher-purpose reason …

I don't.

I can't even say that I was tired of being alone and was on a mission to find my soul mate.

I wasn't.

I didn't even WANT a boyfriend.

I loved being single! And I intended to never marry again! Having married relatively young, I found the "single again" landscape too crazy and "having a man" just wasn't worth the effort and pain.

So why DID I go out with so many guys?

To be blunt, I was nursing a crushed ego.

You see, I had been dating a man, let's call him Mr. Gap-Filler, off-and-on for about a year. I was thrilled when he bought me a very expensive Christmas gift and started doing the things a boyfriend would do (text often, call every night, talk about a future). Imagine my shock when a couple of months later, he announced to one of our networking groups that he'd met the woman he's going to marry – and it wasn't ME! When people were confused, he explained that I was just a "gap–filler" until the real thing came along.

Ouch!!

So I was trying to prove him wrong! Prove that I WAS desirable! And, I'm embarrassed to admit, a small part of me hoped he'd even come back to me (don't judge, y'all!).

The easiest way to do that, so I thought, was to put a profile on Match.com and go out with everyone who asked me. After all, I'd met Mr. Gap-Filler through a brief trial of Match a couple of years prior.

I never saw Mr. Gap-Filler again, but I'm thankful that he was such a jerk. I updated my dormant Match profile and was contacted by over 300 men over about a 4 month period of time. I went out with 24 of them that summer, a total of 49 dates (40 of which are described in this book), and in the process, actually met the love of my life!

I certainly didn't expect to find a husband! I'd tried online dating a few years back and it was the worst experience of my life! Most of the men who contacted me were actually married, stringing me along for months without ever meeting in person. The few I met in person quickly taught me that "normal guys" didn't want a military woman (that's me - 20-plus years career in the Air Force!), and they certainly didn't want a female minister (that's me, too).

Finally, they didn't want a woman who'd only had one sexual partner and minimal dating experience. My first husband was my only partner, and I'd dated very few men since him. I had three strikes against me, and I hadn't even come up to bat yet!

Not only was my online dating experience dismal, at best, but I also noticed that men weren't looking my way like they used to. I thought maybe it was because I was larger than most of the women in my little Midwest town, and asked a couple of platonic guy friends for their opinions. They were in unison: The problem wasn't that I had changed (I hadn't), but that my uniform changed! You see, I had achieved a relatively high rank in the military a few months before all of this went down, and being a busy single mom, I did a lot of my errands in uniform. From my friends' perspective, random men wouldn't feel as comfortable asking me out if they saw me in my uniform, and that's all anyone ever saw me in then.

You may have heard that, "The sexiest thing a woman can put on... is confidence" and that's true! However, there's a difference between being confident and sending clear signals that you will be hard to please. And, apparently, that's what my new rank was saying.

I didn't really have the mindset for marriage anyway! I wanted to prove Mr. Gap- Filler was wrong about my value, but my marriage ended in such a horrible way that I never wanted to be tied down again. You see, I returned home from a six-month military trip to find my house sold and most of my belongings thrown out. We signed divorce papers that week. He went off to enjoy looking young and pulling in college girls. I went off to learn how to be a broke, single mom.

On one hand, life was tough. But on the other, I was free from 15 years of abuse that I had tried to hide under the rug "for the ministry's sake." So I didn't have high expectations of the men I would meet online. I just wanted to meet lots of men and post enough Facebook pictures to make Mr. Gap-Filler jealous.

Fast forward to today: Mr. Man and I are happily married and have a very full life! My oldest son was the result of eight years of work trying to conceive, and after 4 losses, I just *knew* I couldn't have any more children. Mr. Man, himself, had tried for 10 years with his ex-wife and they weren't able to conceive. He had reared her son as his own, the same as he did for mine. So imagine our surprise when we discovered we were pregnant!

While no pregnancy in your 40s is a piece of cake, spending our 1st anniversary with a newborn was worth it! Our two boys are incredibly bonded despite the 10 years between them, and our family just seems to work. We've had a few adjustments to make, and our families too, since I come from an interracial background and he, the Southern Gentleman that he is, most certainly did not.

But you know what? None of this – my life now – would have happened had I not decided to step out of my comfort zone and get back into the dating game. I learned a lot going on all of those dates, and I had a lot of fun, too!

So, I hope you learn a lot from my adventures and have a little fun reading my stories as well!

Blessings,

JJ Conway

Date #1: Mr. Rocker-Turned-Bureaucrat

I was thrilled when the very first man to approach me was a handsome rocker with long hair and a 5-o'clock shadow. His voice was dreamy, and we spent many evenings on the phone engaged in deep, meaningful discussions. He'd recently retired from the military and claimed that he still wanted to live an active life. He liked all of my favorite sports and I quickly said yes when he asked me to dinner. We met at a popular, but not too pricey, local restaurant and it took a while for me to realize that the man pacing outside the restaurant was HIM. Why?

Because the man who approached me did not have long "rocker" hair or carefree appearance. He had a buzz cut. He walked like a bureaucrat. He was a good 60lbs heavier than his profile pic. Talk about bait and switch! This man, clearly looking to meet someone was NOT the man in any of the pictures I saw online. Though disappointed, once I confirmed it was him, I decided to give him a chance. After all, perhaps he recently had surgery or something that packed on the weight. If nothing else, I was broke and this was my one good meal today.

Sadly (or not), things went downhill pretty fast!

Most of the fun outdoor activities he'd described to me were things he'd done 20 years ago. "I can't run, surf, or snowboard now," he explained, "because of my surgeries. And I don't hike or camp anymore because I have sleep apnea and have to sleep connected to a machine."

Sounds horrible, right? But wait. It gets worse!

He had the nerve to tell me I was too broad! "But I'll still give you a chance," he said. "You're in such great shape, I'll overlook your size."

15

This, coming from a guy whose profile pics were thin and trim, yet was sitting there before me with a gut twice my size! Surprisingly, he wanted a 2nd date.

No. Just no.

In retrospect, he'd probably taken his profile pictures right after retiring from the military. He'd probably grown his hair out after 20 years of buzz cuts and wanted to have fun for a few months before taking another job. He probably didn't realize how different he looked, just as I didn't realize how much weight I'd put on after each pregnancy until I looked at pictures people had taken of me.

The victory for me in this story is that in the past, I would have internalized Mr. Rocker-Turned-Bureaucrat's opinions about my size and spent the next couple of weeks hating my appearance. This time, however, I shook it off as HIS problem, something we (as women) need to do a lot more often!

Moral of the Story: *People lie. They put up fake (or really old) profile pictures and dare you to say something. They pretend to be younger than they are, or to enjoy activities they think you want them to enjoy. When you aren't "ok" with the truth, they get mad and lash out at you. Expect it, and don't internalize it as something being wrong with you. It's really something wrong with them.*

Date #2: Mr. Take-Advantage-Of-Me

This sweet, cute, bundle of insecurity let me choose our lunch date location and I chose my favorite lunch spot. It was yummy, and our conversation flowed freely. He had pretty eyes and a kind spirit. Too kind, though. He'd been married too many times for me to list, and he detailed how each one had taken him for a ride! College loans paid off here. A house paid for there. His last wife pressured him for months to retire from the military and buy her a new car. As soon as he did that, she left him!

Thankfully, he didn't have kids with any of these women, or he'd have no hope of retiring with financial stability!

My first thought was, "Wow! I could really get a lot out of this guy!" And after years of give, give, giving with nothing in return, it was really exciting to think I might have someone give to ME for a change.

But then reality crept in and I realized that this guy had a lot of healing to do. I could help him heal, sure, but that's not what I came for! I was looking to have fun, and be carefree, not play counselor, mom, or best friend!

Have you ever noticed that dating profiles that say, "I don't want any drama" tend to attract a lot of drama?

Or that dating profiles that say, "No cheaters" attract a lot of cheaters?

And that dating profiles advertising, "No Gold-Diggers" or "No Men Just Looking for Sex" end up getting exactly those kinds of people?

I'm not an expert, but I think it's because those signals indicate that they've been in those relationships, repeatedly; so while their WORDS say they want one thing, their experience says they'll settle for what they profess NOT to want.

I wished this man the best because he really WAS a nice guy. But I could easily see myself falling into the same pattern as the other women in his life: taking advantage of his good nature and eventually losing respect for him.

Moral of the Story: *If you've been taken advantage of in past relationships, DO NOT broadcast this to your new love interest. At best, you might drive off the "right" kind of partner, and at worse, you might attract predators and users. Mr. Take-Advantage-Of-Me would have been wise to spend a few months working on his own personal growth before seeking another partner.*

Date #3: Mr. Nice-Guy-I-Poofed-On

RTFQ!!! They teach you for college exams: Read the FULL Question! IN this case, RTFP- Read the Full Profile!

I didn't. I was struck by his amazing eyes and he looked like he met all of the "qualifications."

Good-looking... check!

Liked kids... nieces and nephews... check!

Was really into me... check!

So what was the problem? I'm embarrassed to admit that it was my own insecurity that kept me from going on a second date with this 'Nice Guy.' He called and asked several times, but I never responded.

You see, when I first accepted the date, I had several profiles jumbled up in my mind. I expected him to be about a foot taller than he was, and since he was in excellent shape, that meant he was much thinner than I expected.

As you might have guessed from Date #1, I'm no string bean! I'm very fit, but I'm also full-figured and I just knew I wouldn't feel "girly" around someone that size!

A few years prior when I had briefly tried online dating, several of the guys I dated got mad at me for my size. They all started out liking me, but then would criticize my eating and drinking choices, and, ultimately, wanted me to be a better, thinner version of myself. I'd been married to someone like that and I just couldn't expose myself to that kind of negativity again. My feelings would be hurt when guys told me I was too big, even when I tried to post accurate pics and explain before each date that I was broad shouldered.

So even though Date #2 said he was thrilled to meet a "normal" lady on Match.com, I was afraid he would get tired of feeling like he was hugging his mom. And even more so, I wouldn't feel feminine with someone as thin as my own son.

I wish I could have told him that there was nothing wrong with him, but I didn't know how to explain it without hurting his feelings.

Moral of the Story: *Don't judge the man in front of you by the sins of other men who have hurt you. This guy truly deserved at least one more date; he was wonderful! He was everything a lady could want, and I threw away that opportunity because I felt too insecure about my size. Even though it probably wouldn't have lasted, going out a few more times would have both been fun AND boosted both of our dating confidence. He didn't deserve my poofing.*

Date #4: Mr. Gentle-Giant

Divorced female ministers made up a fairly small portion of the population where I lived. The divorced part scared off the "Good Christian Men" and the minister part scared off many of the great guys. Throw in that I'm a tad bit larger than most women in the military and you can understand why I wasn't used to attention from men who looked like Greek gods. When Mr. Gentle-Giant asked me out, I was sure he was setting me up for a scam. This man wasn't just hot... he was HAWT!

I went out with him anyway because, um, did I mention he was haaaawwwwt!? You know what they say: your dating value goes up when you date people of higher caliber!

The scam I expected never came... and I learned a lot from him over the two months that we dated. I noticed he was still active on Match.com, so I continued to accept dates. He was one of only a handful of guys I could actually see a future with.

Our first date was at Starbucks. The other guys I had met with on other dates were easier to connect with because either the restaurant we chose to meet at was empty, or I was the only black woman in the room, so they quickly found me.

But our local Starbucks had a really narrow driveway and it felt awkward standing outside. This usually-empty Starbucks hosted several guys who were sitting alone - just sitting (like they were waiting for someone). I had so much nervous energy because I felt like my date wasn't going to like my appearance: that I had made a good fool of myself asking several guys, "Are you Mr. Gentle-Giant?"

Embarrassed, I went back outside and tried not to get run over while waiting for him to arrive. He was only 5 minutes late, but it felt like an eternity. I had almost left! Sounds silly as I type this, but in the moment, sometimes our emotions and insecurities take over and we expend way too much mental energy on something as minor as where to meet a guy.

Not the car because he'll think I was late.

Don't text "I'm here" because he'll think you're one of "those" strong women.

Don't go back inside because they're all gonna laugh at you!

Don't stand out here looking like a beggar.

It's just too much!

When he walked up 5 minutes later, I was so happy that he actually looked like his profile picture (very rare). And we ended up having a lovely coffee date with easy, yet intelligent conversation.

Moral of the Story: *Don't get so caught up in the small stuff that you miss out on golden opportunities. Although Mr. Gentle-Giant did not win the ultimate prize of becoming Mr. Man, he was a lot of fun to date (and to be seen with!). And for the record, online dating etiquette (yes, there is such a thing) says you should wait outside the restaurant for your date.*

Date #5: Mr. Gentle-Giant at the Park

I really liked Mr. Gentle-Giant, and was excited when he asked if he could see me again. He was fun to talk to and had a lot of business sense and intelligence hidden underneath a magnificent body.

But being broke was cramping my dating style because sitters wanted at least $20/hour plus gas. When you're going out on 2-4 dates a week, you just don't have time or money like that! I had over $800K of divorce debt to pay off, and I had to do what I told my financial planning clients to do: tighten your belt and stop spending money you don't have.

My typical go-to strategy was to ask the guy for a weekday lunch or early dinner date so I could be done before the daycare closed at 6:30. Or for a date during AWANA night since there was no program for adults, and I wouldn't feel guilty for dropping my son off to go on a date. On occasion, there would be "mother's night out," or "mother's day out" events on the weekend and I used those as well. Every so often, my friends would watch my son for me as well. They were all single themselves, so I tried not to impose too much.

Mr. Gentle-Giant and I had to be creative about spending time together because it was tough meeting during the day.

Being in the restaurant business, his work schedule didn't cooperate with a lot of daytime or early evening dates, so we planned some Saturday mornings at the park.

The idea was that he'd bring his kids to play at the park, and I'd bring my son to play at the park. We were just two parents sitting on the bench talking while our kids played with each other and whoever else was at the park. The children had no idea we were dating. My son still asks to hang out with his son to this day.

Moral of the Story: *Be creative! Find ways to get out there and date that don't hurt your financial or family bottom line. Don't kill yourself or your pocketbook just to get a date. A man is not worth going into debt for! He's not worth sneaking out of work for (and possibly getting fired from your job). He's not worth sacrificing your commitments to family and community. If it's meant to be, you'll find a way to make it work with the money and time you have available.*

Date #6: Mr. Chutzpah

I still remember how flattered I was when Mr. Chutzpah chased me down in the Sam's Club and asked me out to dinner. It was kind of awkward and he wasn't my type. I liked barrel-chested, broad men on the shorter end of the scale. Mr. Chutzpah was the right height, but he was more like a strong fox than the big bear I was going for. I'd just finished reading *What Southern Women Know About Flirting*, and had decided to internalize one of the great lessons in that book: always reward a man who is gentlemanly with a big smile; if you are single, and a man has the boldness to ask you to dinner, then GO!

You see, in today's world, it can be difficult for a man to put himself out there like that. I remember insisting I could open my own doors and scowling when a man complimented my appearance. Modern, strong, independent women can be intimidating and it takes a lot of gumption for a man to ask us out anymore.

In short, even though you might not be interested in the man, giving him a chance will encourage him to ask the next lady for a date. So please consider going out with every man who directly asks you out to dinner, especially if you don't have anything better going on.

So when Mr. Chutzpah asked me out, I was coming out of a dry spell! Yes, men on Match.com were approaching me like crazy, but typically lost interest when they discovered my high rank in the military. Believe it or not, I started telling guys whom I actually wanted a date with that I did "admin work" so that I could at least get to know them before I dropped the truth on them. As I mentioned in the intro, in the months since my promotion, no one had asked me out in person.

So here I was, standing in my uniform, with this scrappy, wiry Cajun telling me how beautiful I was and that he would regret it forever if he didn't ask me on a date. That kind of boldness deserved at least one dinner with a gorgeous woman and that's exactly what I gave him.

Mr. Chutzpah encouraged me to try something new, so we went to a popular sushi restaurant. We had a fantastic conversation! I had so much fun that I kept trying to imagine ways to make things work with him. Unfortunately, our lifestyles were too different for a good partnership and I couldn't wish that away.

That night, I expanded my culinary repertoire and gained a great friend. Our conversation and social media interactions over the years has been wonderful.

Moral of the Story: *When a man asks you out, unless there are serious quality issues or you're already seeing someone, consider saying "yes!" You'll encourage him to keep approaching quality women like yourself (which is good for the overall sisterhood), you increase your "dating value" in the eyes of men around you (by being on a date) and you never know what you might learn!*

Date #7: Mr. Strong-And-Sensitive

I opened up my Match.com inbox to find an email titled, "Our Story."

Keep in mind that my handle was "SavedP."

It went like this:

> Strong-And-Sensitive: viewed your profile
> SavedP: viewed my profile
> Strong-And-Sensitive: winked
> SavedP: winked back
> Strong-And-Sensitive said: Helloooo!!!! I'm Strong-And-Sensitive...
> SavedP said: Helloooo!!! I'm _____(please insert name here) (wait.... Hold on that's not rite...) hummmm...... (I got it I will use your user name) (ok from the top)
>
> Strong-And-Sensitive: viewed your profile
> SavedP: viewed my profile
> Strong-And-Sensitive: winked
> SavedP: winked back
> Strong-And-Sensitive said: Helloooo!!!! I'm Strong-And-Sensitive
> SavedP said: Helloooo!!!! I'm savedP
> FFW>>>> 2 or 3 years...
> The happy couple get married
> FFW>>>> 20 or 30 years...
> Happily ever after... The END...

NONE of the 300+ guys who contacted me that summer sent me a first email like THAT!

I wasn't too thrilled with his profile picture (or his grammar), but I just HAD to meet this man. And I'm glad I did. He was dreamy! Short, but stacked, and was the perfect balance of

Tough Guy and Sensitive Soul. He owned a construction company and was also very creative in writing and art. I fell hard for this one!

We had an amazing first date and quickly set up a second. For those who are counting, yes, I was still seeing Mr. Gentle-Giant. However, he continued to be active on Match.com and we weren't "boyfriend-girlfriend."

One thing I learned from my first experience on Match.com was that you are never actually "exclusively dating" someone until you both - no-kidding - talk about it and make that decision. No exclusivity convo? Then don't assume he's only dating you.

Moral of the Story: *Please don't turn down an opportunity to meet someone new if your current love interest has not made your status "official" because quality partners could be passing you by! And please don't dismiss a guy just because his grammar is atrocious (more on this later)!*

Date #8: Mr. Gentle-Giant Teaches Me What "Watch a Movie" Really Means

Are you an experienced dater? If so, you can skip this chapter! I wasn't. In fact, I had one boyfriend in high-school, two in college and married the second one. We both went to a military college, which made it difficult to do the traditional dating thing. I had no idea what I was getting into when I tried to date online in my late 30s!

I had no idea that in online dating vernacular, "Come over and watch a movie," does NOT mean watch a movie.

Just like I didn't know that when someone writes on their profile, or in their messages to you that they like to "hang out," they are basically talking about sex.

Or that writing "I'm looking for clean fun," doesn't mean what I intended (we're going to out to dinner and do other non-sexual things). Instead, it means to many online daters that 'I've got proof that I'm STD-free.'

Most of these lessons I learned through men who didn't earn a date with me. I'll spare you the whole story of how Mr. Gentle-Giant taught me what "Come over and watch a movie" really means, and just skip to how it ends: with him storming angrily out of my apartment.

"But I told you I was coming over to watch a movie! What else did you expect?!"

I certainly didn't expect what HE expected!

Moral of the Story: *If you're recently single again, you might want to check out a few dating books or recent dating movies to get a handle on what people actually mean. Or talk to some older teens/young adults. It can be humbling. I got* *my church young adults to talk about their adventures in dating; I learned a lot! I highly recommend all of the ladies in my singles group read through a few Pick-Up-Artists (PUA) websites to learn about PUA strategies, like "negging," where a man insults a woman hoping it will make her want to prove she's awesome.*

I also recommend that if anyone reading this has lived a sheltered life (like I had), that they regularly visit websites for men such as AskMen.com (an advice site for men). These sites, blogs and books expanded my insight into the male psyche and allowed me to nip untoward behavior in the bud. Even church men are still *men* and these sites helped me a lot!

Date #9: Mr. Cool-Biker-Dude

Biker Dude.

Single Dad. I mean, a *real* single dad who has his kids most of the time.

Good-looking man with an easy southern drawl.

I couldn't wait for our lunch date!

The big day arrived and I realized I'd forgotten to bring civilian clothes to change into. I didn't want to meet him in uniform. As I mentioned earlier, my rank and position in the Air Force turned most guys off, so I wanted to get to know them before divulging that information. My experience might be different from yours; for me, it seemed like guys wanted a woman to *have* a job, but not have a high-paying job. It seemed like guys wanted their date to have a little income, but not earn more than they did.

I began to stress out about making a good first impression. There was a Walmart across the street from the restaurant, so I ran in to see if I could quickly grab an outfit.

Note to self: One does not "quickly go into Walmart" for anything. I found something, but the lines were long and I realized that if I didn't leave soon, I would be late. We only had an hour, so I put back the clothes and rushed over. And, of course, the intersection conspired against me with red lights and an accident, and it was 15 minutes past our meet time when I finally showed up.

Imagine what he saw: a frazzled, stressed out, military woman with a ton of frustrated, negative energy.

Do you think Mr. Cool-Biker-Dude ever asked me out again?

Of course not!

We're friends now, happily in our own relationships, and we can laugh about it, but at the time, I was devastated! My negative vibe was so strong that I lost with him the moment I walked through the door.

Moral of the Story: *Whether you are laid back or more "Type A" like me, I highly recommend doing your best to RELAX when on a date! If you're looking for a fun, easy-going guy, being stressed and frazzled might accidentially push him away. Plan your days and dates out in advance so that you can just be in the moment and focus on enjoying yourself on the date. The more you enjoy yourself, the more likely it is that he'll enjoy YOU!*

Date #10: Mr. Who-Is-THAT?!

I was already bored 5 minutes into some meeting when a tall piece of fine chocolate walked into the room.

"Who is THAT?!" I thought to myself. I'd never been so mesmerized by someone in uniform. Being a military gal, I've seen the worst side of military men and, quite frankly, wasn't interested in any of 'em. Until now.

He sat down next to me.

He smelled good.

How distracting!

When he finally spoke, it was with a soft-yet-stern voice. His air of authority silenced everyone, and his observations were spot-on. I don't even remember the outcome of the meeting. I just know I had to meet him. But he was late, the meeting itself had run late, and I had to hustle back to my office or I was going to be late for my boss.

I've always believed the old adage that you shouldn't pursue a man, but I just had to find this guy and spend time with him. He might just be the reason all these other guys weren't really working out!

I'd tracked him down and began to build a business relationship with him; the more I learned about him, the more I liked what I saw. Bolstered by my online dating success, I figured I had nothing to lose and asked if he wanted to hang out with me one night. I didn't call it a "date" per se, but something more along the lines of:

"My friend bailed on our plans (which was true). I've already committed to childcare and don't want to cancel on a good sitter at the last minute (which was true). And I don't want to go alone so would you like to hang out at the Boardwalk with me?"

We had a lovely time at dinner and our conversation flowed freely! It was like we were old friends.
I just knew he was going to ask me out "for real this time."

But he didn't.

We saw each other sometimes at work, laughed and joked.

We even chatted on the phone about music/poetry, but still, no date.

This normally wouldn't have been a problem, except that I kept thinking of that first meal as a date when in his mind it was nothing of the sort. While my imagination was running wild with dreams of a world-changing relationship with this man, he was off looking for his own dates.

Moral of the Story: *When an alpha male really wants you, he will pursue. I've heard a lot of guys say women need to make the first move, but when I dug into this, I learned that they almost always mean don't mean "ask him out." They mean: smile, make conversation, and give him "It's ok to ask me out" signals. Unless you prefer taking the initiative in all areas of your relationship, I would recommend against asking men out. You might have fun, but you'll never know if he really was interested or just filling some empty time.*

Date #11: Mr. Gentle-Giant Finally Blurts It Out

I was the first woman Mr. Gentle-Giant asked out on Match.com. I was a breath of fresh air after a miserable, sexless marriage. I was great with his difficult kids, understood the dynamics of his business and liked his favorite shows. These were all things he craved in his marriage.

I was all that he needed!

For about 3 weeks.

When his Match.com profile pic changed to one of him shirtless, I knew the end was near. He was on there constantly, didn't call as often, and though we had fun together, I felt something was off.

So I asked him.

And he told me that he really enjoyed spending time with me, but he really wanted a more attractive woman.

"Excuse me?"

"I really like you," he said, pulling up my Match.com profile, "but where is the woman in your pictures?? She's hot!"

"That IS me! The only difference is you've been seeing me during the week and not all dressed up for a night out!"

We then made plans to go out for a fancy dinner that Saturday. We both got dressed up and had a lovely time.

What I didn't realize until years later is that I'm one of those people who look much better in pictures than in real life. It's great to be able to pose and make ourselves look thinner and more beautiful, but if a man is disappointed in our appearance, it can be harder to win his heart!

I thought I looked the same. Not to him.

Like it or not, I had to accept the fact that looks are important to him. And guess what I discovered? In the years since this dating spree, I've talked to MANY men who feel the same: a woman's appearance affects greatly his affections for her.

Moral of the Story: *Men tend to be visual and most that I've talked to when running my singles groups said they care first about appearance before appreciating the finer points of a woman's personality. When a man falls in love with profile pictures that aren't accurate, it may be harder for him to fall in love with the real-world you, especially if he thinks he can land someone more attractive. Remember: we are more successful in relationships when the other person feels good about themselves around us. While we are NOT responsible for someone's reaction to our appearance, it's helpful to keep in mind that looks really DO matter.*

Date #12: Bye, Mr. Strong-And-Sensitive

Mr. Strong-And-Sensitive and I had one of the most fun second dates I can remember. We went to an MMA fight.

I always hated when my dad watched the fights on TV. Boooooooooring! So why did I go to an MMA fight?

Because I lived in an area where there wasn't much to do in the evenings that didn't involve smoking and alcohol. Plus, I had friends who were going, and it would be an easy way for them to check him out.

It was fun!! I did not expect to have so much fun watching people beat each other up (don't judge y'all)!

Apparently, I got really into it because he said later that he didn't know what was more entertaining: the fight, or watching me cheer on my chosen competitor.

We went with my group of friends to dinner and I guess I got a little too comfortable because I accidently ruined everything!

You see, I had several go-to statements I would give a guy when I never wanted to see him again. About 80% of men lost interest when they found out I was a scientist in the Air Force. And for the handful that were still interested after that, my trump card was telling them, "I'm a minister."

We got to talking at dinner and one of my friends pulled out a minister's credentials that she'd obtained from an internet church. Forgetting my date, I pulled out my minister's card from Church of the Living God and showed it to her. The look of shock and horror on Mr. Strong-and-Sensitive's face spoke volumes.

I was not surprised when he unfriended me on Facebook and never asked me out again.

Moral of the Story: *There's nothing wrong with being a physicist or a minister. It's who I am, and I'm not going to change for a man. However, we have to be aware of and adjust for the culture of available men. The fun loving guys I'm attracted to aren't looking for a physicist (OR a minister). If I led with those things, they might never get to know me well enough to fall in love with me. Another lesson learned: don't lose your self-control! While it ultimately wouldn't have worked out, I would rather our relationship end because we weren't a good fit, not because I forgot about him and divulged information that I should have kept close-hold for a few more dates.*

Date #13: Mr. Gentle-Giant, Stalker

I'm a firm believer that you shouldn't cancel your pre-existing plans upon meeting a new beau. For one, I don't want a man to feel like he's super important in my life until he's proven himself to be worthy. When we first meet, I'm looking for a man who is working hard to win our faithfulness. Canceling all of my "Girls Night Out" could make him feel like he already won and doesn't need to try so hard anymore.

My experience has been that most people value what they work for rather than what's freely given.

Also, having come from an abusive relationship, I'm wary of any motivation or pressure to minimize time spent with others. Cancelling pre-existing plans can potentially send the "I have no life and no friends" signal that is attractive to predators. How willing we are to do this can also be a dangerous precedent that makes us susceptible to abusive relationships.

One of a controlling person's best tricks is to slowly pressure us into no longer having contact with our friends and family. Eventually we become isolated. The controlling partner becomes our world.

So when Mr. Gentle-Giant wanted to go out on our sports-fellowship day, I told him I already had plans. If it had been the other way around, I would have asked questions to see if he was telling the truth or playing the field, so I didn't think anything of him asking for details…until he showed up!

He said he wasn't there to participate or hang out. He explained that he didn't believe I was telling the truth and wanted to see for himself! We took one of my favorite pictures that night, and I was so thrilled at how good we looked together that I missed the red flag at first. But then, the more I thought about it, the more uncomfortable I became with the idea that he felt the need to "check on" me. We're not even "boyfriend – girlfriend" and you're getting jealous/territorial? You're out there dating on Match.com (please don't ask me how I knew this) and yet I can't have a day out with friends?

Imagine what life would be like if we WERE a couple!

Moral of the Story: It's a huge "Red flag" when a man can't trust you, or thinks you're cheating or lying when you've never given him reason to. Worst case, he could be very controlling and/or abusive. In this case, Mr. Gentle-Giant probably just had some issues to work out before he could be a good partner for me.

Date #14: Mr. You-Owe-Me

Remember that old saying, "If it seems too good to be true, it probably is?"

When Mr. You-Owe-Me first approached me on Match.com, I thought he'd made a mistake. A high-ranking flyboy from an upstanding family, he looked like he'd stepped off the cover of *People Magazine*. I'd seen him around before, and he just didn't strike me as the type that would enjoy hanging out with little ol' me.

I was still building up my bruised ego, and was confident that Mr. Gap-Filler was stalking my Facebook page. After seeing all of the pictures I had posted (me with a string of successful, good-looking men), I just knew he was regretting his decision to break up with me. He was probably crying himself to sleep every night, and a few pics with Mr. You-Owe-Me would be icing on the cake.

Before I continue, let me just say that from the perspective of the men who attended my singles groups, it's very, VERY, unlikely that a man who breaks up with one woman to date another will be crying, or even THINKING, about that woman. He generally moves on because he perceives his new love to be of higher quality, makes him look better, or is more of a fit for his lifetime goals. He's unlikely to stalk your Facebook page while that relationship is intact. So my recommendation in these cases is to move on, find someone else, and let your revenge be "a life well lived."

But I didn't know that then.

So I said yes and asked Mr. You-Owe-Me if he wanted to meet. He suggested three restaurants I could pick from, and they were the finest restaurants in town! I was impressed.

Another thing I didn't know back then? There's a reason he wanted to impress me with those exclusive restaurants.

At dinner, he encouraged me to talk about my favorite topics, but eventually I noticed that he wasn't really listening. Those of you with experience probably know where this was going. Please keep in mind that up 'til this "summer of love," I'd only had maybe 9 other dates in my entire life.

I was so disappointed to discover that night Mr. You-Owe-Me couldn't care less about who I was and what I liked. In his eyes, I was an easy target: a naïve, older woman who probably didn't get much male attention and would likely acquiesce to his every demand.

Moral of the Story: *When a guy lets you choose from one of the most expensive restaurants in town, watch out. Notice if he's actively engaged in conversation or just trying to lower your guard. He may be trying to impress you, and most likely wants something afterward.*

Date #15: Mr. Not-Too-Young-After-All

My quest to go out with everyone who asked was lots of fun! Experiences like those with Mr. You-Owe-Me notwithstanding, I was trying all kinds of new restaurants and activities, and boosting my ego as well.

I highly recommend going out with everyone who asks, but there were plenty of young guys that I'm glad never asked me to dinner.

For example, the one who asked if my old bones could handle him.

Or the one who said he could teach an old dog new tricks.

And my personal favorite: the young man who thought I was a freak because I'd only had one sexual partner (my ex-husband) and wasn't inclined to have any more unless we were married.

I learned quickly to dismiss men who asked sexual questions since that wasn't my focus; so very few younger men even made it to getting my number.

When Mr. Not-Too-Young-After-All approached me, he looked kind of young, but respectful enough that I gave him a chance.

When I saw him in person, my heart soared! His profile looked like he was in his 20s, but he was in his late 30s.

Stop and think about that for a second.

I didn't think about it until later.

You have to know that you don't look like you did 10 years ago.

You have to know that even if you keep yourself fit and trim, you STILL don't look the same as you did in pictures 10 years ago.

Our lunch was fun, but he clearly wanted a younger woman. He eventually found her (and I was flattered that she looked similar to me, skin tone and all). I moved on and found someone who was more comfortable with their age.

Moral of the Story: *A lot of guys post younger pictures of themselves. Expect it. Don't be too surprised. The issue here is you have to uncover why they posted pictures that clearly aren't them. Sometimes we don't realize how we've aged. Some men have told me that when they see a man with a much younger woman, they know there's an underlying ego problem. My experience agrees with this.*

Date #16: Mr. Cub

By now you've seen that one of my biggest lessons learned is that people don't look like their profile pictures. Most of the time, they use pictures that make them look younger and thinner, but sometimes, I was pleasantly surprised.

Mr. Cub was one of those surprises.

His profile pic sported an open collar, with chest hair peeking out, and a gold chain.

Can you say stereotypical "Rico Suave" dirt bag??

But I was committed to going out with everyone who asked and that's how I found myself at lunch sitting across from one of the nicest young men I've had the pleasure of spending time with.

Even though he was younger, he had his act together as a man and father; he loved my Jesus, and I found myself very attracted to him. He was a reservist who was trying to transition into full-time civilian employment and create a more stable life for himself and his kids.

I was concerned about him being in the reserves because the military has strict rules about dating between ranks. And, ultimately, that's why we never went out again. Oh sure! We scheduled dates, but each one had something crazy force a cancellation.

Babysitter flaked.

Car accident.

Tree fell on the house.

After a while, we both got the cosmic hint that we were not meant to be. We'd run into each other on occasion and even though there was a mutual attraction, we both knew it would go nowhere.

Moral of the Story: *First of all, don't judge someone's appearance (good or bad) until you see him in person! He looked creepy in his profile picture, yet in real life, he had amazing eyes and was very handsome! Another lesson with Mr. Cub is that just because you're both great people doesn't mean you're great for each other. And finally, if someone keeps cancelling, consider moving on. While it could be a coincidence… and it could be true… outlandish stories of why a date has to cancel generally mean the relationship itself isn't going to work. Even if the excuses are true, there was something in his life attracting all that drama (as if his non-conscious manifested reasons for us to not date). More likely, he didn't really want to go out, but wanted to reassure himself I was still interested.*

Date #17: Mr. Won't-Pay-Child-Support

My date with Mr. Cub kicked off my craziest adventure yet: four dates in one week!

I was approached by over 300 men in the couple of months I was on Match.com. I ignored the obviously sexual approaches. For everyone else, my strategy was to only give as much effort as they gave me. So "hey" emails were answered back with "hey." If the man wrote a paragraph, then I wrote one back to him. If he wrote one sentence, I didn't spend hours crafting a 2-page response. Otherwise, I would have been angry at pouring time and energy into a man who never reciprocated.

For each new man, I created a document with their online info, our messages and notes about them. This worked fine for 2-3 dates a week, but the week I went on four dates, my brain got overloaded and I began to mix up the details!

When this tall, broad shouldered, pony-tailed biker who loves Jesus started chatting with me, I was instantly smitten! Our dates revolved around his community activities, and it's hard to describe them without compromising his identity. Let's just say we had a lot of fun for three dates while staying in line with my boundaries and ministry!

The deal-breaker? He didn't pay his child support, and no-kidding, he asked me to pray that God would take the responsibility from him! It was only about $100/mo. That's nothing! He had money to pay for all of the fun things we did, so I didn't feel sorry for him in the least! I already learned my lesson from being married to someone who was financially irresponsible: People spend their money on what's important to them. Clearly a responsibility to his children wasn't important to him.

We never went out again.

It's easier to cut someone loose when you have plenty of other options to go out with, and as much as I enjoyed his company I had to cut him loose. Having this kind of flexibility is another big reason I recommend going out with everyone who asks you unless there's a huge deal breaker!

For example, if a man asked me to do something illegal (like the one who asked me to get him some military gear) or outside of my boundaries, I wouldn't do it. But if they were the only dogs barking up my tree, then I suppose I would be more tempted to accept low-quality and disrespectful behavior. Being open to more types of men meant more dates. And more dates meant I wasn't as stressed if the current one didn't work out.

I learned there is a limit to "more dates," however! After being embarrassed after asking one date about his grandma's surgery (when it was another of my four dates concerned about the surgery) and someone else's trip to Las Vegas (when it was another man who travelled), I realized four dates in one week was just too much for me.

Moral of the Story: *Just 'cuz he's good-looking and lots of fun doesn't mean he's right for YOU. Be willing to face the red flags for what they are. All too often, we overlook these signals because we are so excited to have romance in our lives. Or we stuff those nagging feelings that something is "off" because we don't want to mess up a good thing. Guess what? The best you'll see of someone is in the early stages of dating when they're trying to impress you. So please don't ignore those feelings.*

Date #18: Mr. I'm-Just-Testing-You

Before I became single again, I used to run with a fantastic group. One of my friends would entertain us with stories of his dating the night before. He was the ultimate bachelor – plenty of money, gregarious, handsome - so he had plenty of fun stories!

Eventually, I noticed a pattern to his dates. Everyone had to pass the "Don't let me get in your pants on the first couple of dates," test and the "I'll casually bring up marriage, but if she talks too much about it, she'll never get a second date" test.

The next level was the "Arrive at a hard-to-find restaurant on time" test and the "You thought this was a date? No, we're just watching the game at a sports bar" test.

Very few women made it to the "Meet my friends at a bar" test, the first hint that he actually wanted a relationship with her. Unfortunately, on the next date, also with his friends, she'd still have to pass the "Stay cool when I didn't save you a seat at the table" test.

When Mr. I'm-Just-Testing-You immediately tried to push my boundaries, I lumped him in with all of the other jerks who did things like grab my behind on the first date and then blow up angrily when I cut them off with, "You haven't earned booty grabbing privileges yet." Or invite women friends who showed up at our restaurant to sit in our booth on either side of him.

What surprised me about Mr. I'm-Just-Testing-You is that he eventually told me that's what he was doing. I'd passed the test, but it was clear my ministry and his lifestyle weren't compatible. We talked about it for a bit. I thought he was just full of himself, but the guys in my singles group confirmed his actions: men test women all of the time.

To earn a man's respect, we need to hold fast to our boundaries and what we say is important to us. This is especially true for men who feel a bit inferior on the inside because they will test a woman, and when she acquiesces, they'll use that as an excuse to stop dating her. Mr. I'm-Just-Testing-You said he felt like the Groucho Marx quote, "I wouldn't be a member of any club that would accept me!"

It's easy to read that and say, "Then I don't want him anyway!" but if most men are testing like this, then that mindset might lead to a lot of lonely nights. Instead, I recommend women daters spend time defining who they are, where their boundaries lie and then be firm about it. At the same time, being patient with a man who tests (but otherwise meets your requirements) could lead to a fantastic future with a great guy! Mr. I'm-Just-Testing-You is now married to someone who, like me, didn't pass all of his tests but captured his heart. They are very happy!

Moral of the story: *Occasionally, testers are looking for prey or booty calls, but more often, they, like my running group friend, aren't even aware they've set up a series of hoops no partner can possibly jump through. It's a self-protection mechanism. Humans are frail and fragile, and when things don't work out, remember, it's probably not you - it really could be HIM. It could be HIS insecurities, HIS failings, or any number of internal struggles HE might have. Not YOU. So please consider giving a tester another chance, especially if that's the only deal-breaker. He just may need time to feel worthy of you!*

Date #19: Mr. Gas-Station

One of most bizarre "dates" happened outside of a gas station outside of Atlanta.

Mr. Gas-Station and I were supposed to meet while I was in Atlanta for a week-long church conference. One thing led to another, and we kept cancelling and rescheduling.

You might remember from Mr. Cub that when there's too many cancellations, I stop being invested in a man. Even if I might still make plans, I'll expect that they, too, will be cancelled and have a Plan B for that evening.

Plus, I had a lot of dates already lined up for when I got back from the conference - four more weeks of them actually! Who cared if I missed out on one guy who couldn't find a way to make our lunch date happen!

As I drove home from Atlanta, I got a curious text from Mr. Gas-Station asking if I was still in town and if we could meet. When I told him I was on the road already, he asked if I could meet him at a particular truck stop that was on his way home and also on my way out of town. I had to get gas and snacks anyway, so I agreed, fully expecting him to stand me up.

Only he was there.

Ummm… wow!

Leaning against his truck, with smooth caramel biceps bulging out from under his work polo sleeves, I took in his big smile, wavy hair and felt like maybe it's really true that "Good things come to those who wait."

We had a lovely chat and he called me as I drove back home. The conversation was great until he said he couldn't stand church girls.

"You do realize," I reminded him, "I was here for a week-long church conference. That kind of makes me a church girl."

He texted later to apologize, said he'd never met anyone like me and didn't know church girls could be so amazing. We chatted, but then he made some snide remark about religious women! Again, I called him on it. The next couple of times he texted me, I wrote back, "Is this the guy who texted me, a minister, that he didn't like church girls?"

Moral of the Story: *When someone shows you who they are, believe them the first time. Don't keep trying to make a poor fit work just because you're lonely or because being seen with that person would make you look good. Whether he was just dumb or playing pick-up games, he wasn't right for ME!*

Date #20: The Night I Meet Mr. Man

My schedule was jam-packed and I was getting to the point where I didn't care about proving myself anymore. My schedule was booked for the next few weeks and I felt very desirable.

I also had orders to deploy, and there was a very good chance that when I returned, the Air Force would move me to another state. I was asking for the D.C. area where I thought the culture and quality of men would be higher than my little Midwest town. After two months of online dating, I was considering getting into a relationship again, but since long distance relationships don't generally work out, I wasn't expecting to meet the love of my life until I got to D.C.

So when Mr. Man originally wrote me, I was just accepting dates to have fun. His message to me was very simple, but it had grammar issues and he didn't even give his message a title! Match.com just used his first line:

> MSG: Hi,,,,you came up on my daily matches and after...

> Hi,,,,you came up on my daily matches and after looking at your profile I feel we have some things in common. I'd like to get to know more about you. I too am not looking to rush into anything, so maybe we can just start here and see where it goes. Hope to hear from you soon.

Yes. That. Was. His. Message. Bad punctuation and all. How many of you would have just automatically hit "delete?" I already wasn't impressed by his message, and his profile stated that he was a musician, which was another strike against him. I had divorced one of those and didn't need another, so I have to admit, I wasn't exactly very encouraging to him.

He quickly got my number and asked when we could meet. I still felt like any man who took the time out to ask me on a date should get one, but I was booked with dates and travel for the next five weeks.

"Next Friday night," I told him. "I promised my friend I'd support her church singles game night. If you can make it, great! Otherwise, we can set something up in about 5 weeks."

He said he would be there.

I wasn't too thrilled about his "old guy" outfit (worn Tommy Hilfiger polo with jeans) when he did show up at the church, but it *was* a game night, and we *did* say we'd be casual. And while I'm an "equal opportunity employer," I wasn't so sure he'd be a good fit for my multi-racial family.

Even so, he had a distinguished air about him, was very tall and broad shouldered like me, and while clearly a professional, could be goofy and fun in the moment. My head was still swimming with all of the other date potentials in my line-up, but he definitely would get a second date!

Because of how broad and strong I am, Mr. Man was one of few men I could stand or sit next to and still feel very feminine. I definitely saw us getting physical. I checked out his hands and feet, and then mentally chastised myself for being a minister thinking about sex in a church.

I enjoyed his easy conversation and we seemed to like many of the same games and shows. We left there and went to his favorite steakhouse where he treated me to a lovely meal. We closed the place down and then searched for another place to hang out until THAT closed. Finally, at about 4 a.m., it was time to go home.

He set up a second date before we left, and we continued setting up each date before we finished the last.

However, I knew that I'd be deploying in two months, so I didn't put much stock into him. Fortunately, he knew what he wanted: Me! And he wasn't about to just let me go!

Moral of the story: *Give every guy who approaches you a chance. I've said it often because it bears repeating! His profile may not portray him in the best light. His messages might be getting garbled by that infamous autocorrect. He may just be a goofy guy who doesn't know how to present an online image.*

Women in my singles groups tell me that if a man doesn't write more than a few sentences, or talk about her profile in great depth, or if he has grammatical or spelling errors, then she doesn't respond. I say respond anyway! If he writes you a sentence, write one back. If he says, "hey," write him back, "hey," and see where things lead. The only way I cut men off was if they got sexual too fast or disrespected my faith. Other than that, I responded in kind until they stopped reaching out. And it worked for me!

Maybe you don't like his job? Give him a chance anyway! Mr. Man is a bonafide "gets paid" musician, and I feel very strongly that secular music erodes a preacher's anointing. Once we discussed it, he never bothered me with it, and still doesn't.

And finally, to my sistas waiting for that church-grown, anointed, wavy-haired brotha, give EVERY man a chance. He may not have the style, anointing, or entourage you always imagined would be at your side, but he just might be exactly what you need! I've taken a lot of flak for Mr. Man being: a) is outside of my race and b) not in ministry.

I started out trying to date men of the cloth, but the youth pastors and the associate ministers were pushiest about sex. I tried to date men who looked like my son, but most of them did not want me. Out of 100+ brothas who approached me, I only went out with two (plus Mr. Who-is-THAT) because they told me they didn't want a black woman (thought I was Latina). Or that I wasn't subservient enough to properly appreciate a professional black man who was interested in me when he could have any black woman he wanted.

Not only did Mr. Man meet me at a church for our first date, but he is one of only two other men I dated to actually attend church service with me. The other, also outside my race, owned two bars and a comedy club. So please, ladies, give every man a chance!

Date #21: Mr. Gentle-Giant Turns Out To Be Married

I had a good time with Mr. Man, but I still had several dates lined up. Working in a male-dominated environment, I'd heard enough men talk about how they multi-date that I knew never to stop dating unless there's an "exclusivity" conversation.

Next in my queue was Mr. Gentle-Giant. Thought I'd already seen some red flags, our kids got along well and I mostly enjoyed being around him.

Years ago, when I first dabbled in online dating, I was approached by MANY men who were still married. Even guys who told me they were divorced lied! I would get to know them only to find out that they hadn't even filed divorce papers!

So rather than ask if they were divorced, I started asking if the court had processed their divorce decree yet. Being military, I dated in many states. In most states, a court-stamped decree typically meant they were divorced.

But not in all states! I learned this the hard way because Mr. Gentle-Giant was from a jurisdiction with laws I wasn't used to. He'd been to court. The judge had processed his decree. He was paying child support. And yet, one day while watching a movie (for real this time - he remembered my boundaries), he started talking about how his divorce would be final in a couple months. WHAT?? He technically wasn't single?!

I was so angry! He got angry that I got angry. After all, he was honest with me and it wasn't his fault I moved every two years and didn't understand how this state worked. I am so very thankful we hadn't crossed any intimacy boundaries!

From that point on, I told him we could hang out with the singles group and get to know each other, but I wasn't going to be alone with him until he was officially single.

While I wish I'd have been more patient with him, it really didn't matter in the great scheme of things. By time I figured things out, I was already dating Mr. Man! And, as you'll soon see, Mr. Man is perfect for me.

Moral of the Story: If you care about your date being "Divorced," and not just "Separated," make sure you understand the law. And ask specifically if they're single. Don't dance around it. Make your opinion clear. But also give grace and look for creative solutions that don't violate your boundaries if the situation isn't ideal. You can get to know someone without "dating" them or putting yourself in a compromising situation.

Date #22: Must Learn To Trust My Gut!

It was dumb, dumb, dumb for me to accept this date that wasn't really a date with a man who already showed me his true colors! I should have been spending time on myself, or looking for a man that I could actually see myself in a relationship with. If nothing else, I should have remembered the 3-Day-Rule: you are not available sooner than three days out. Even if your "plans" are suddenly washing your hair and cleaning your kitchen, if a man asks you out on the spur of the moment, you explain that you already have plans. Supposedly, this increases your value in their eyes, and helps prevent you from being relegated to booty-call status.

While the bulk of the guys in my singles groups dismissed this as "playing games," I must note that they tended to disrespect the women who were always instantly available. Sorry, ladies.

Mr. You-Owe-Me calls me up and says he wants to go check out an historical site. He didn't want to go alone, it wasn't the kind of trip you invited male friends to and he didn't want to ask any of his new lady-friends (yes, plural) because they might think it as a pre-lude to a relationship. He remembered I liked that kind of stuff, hoped I would tag along and figured he could count on me not to pressure him for anything "relationshippy" afterward.

Sure, why not? Another man had cancelled that day's date, and I wanted to be truthful with Mr. Man about my schedule being jam-packed. After all, I'd used my schedule being packed for the next couple weeks to motivate Mr. Man to come to the church event, and I didn't want him to think I'd been a liar. Even though Mr. You-Owe-Me was jerky last time, he was making it very clear we were friends and this wasn't a date.

Spending time with him in friend mode was MUCH more fun than spending time with him on date mode. He was actually very interesting to talk to, and this other side of him was very attractive. I was actually a little sad that he wasn't acting more into me and that I felt no sexual tension whatsoever! There were certain romantic-looking spots at the site, and since we were the only two visitors, I tried to get close to him to see if he'd make a move. Still nothing! We were just friends, as if he didn't notice my openers.

Fast forward six hours, and it was time to go home. We stopped at a local joint and ordered our food. His energy changed as we were standing in line. He grabbed my hand as I was about to pay and said he'd cover it. I felt led to say, "No, that's ok," but didn't want to offend him. As we ate, his suave side came out more and more. Something seemed off, but I couldn't put my finger on it. Why was I being so foolish? Just few hours ago, I was trying to GET him to make a move. I should have been thrilled that he was "into me" again, but instead, by the time we arrived at my apartment, I had become extremely uncomfortable.

Before I could get out of the car, he leaned over to kiss me, catching me by surprise and holding me incredibly tight.

"I thought you weren't interested in me like that!"

"I'm complicated that way," he responded as he leaned in for another kiss. He began whispering how beautiful I was and how amazing it was just to be his real self with me as he kissed up and down my neck. I might have fallen for the act, except he was holding me so tight I couldn't move. Clearly, this wasn't about a budding relationship!

I still don't remember exactly how I got out of there with my dignity intact (but GOD!), but I do recall getting called a string of names for "leading him on," and I was quite shook up afterward.

Moral of the Story: *Trust your gut. My gut told me not to let him pay and I could see in his eyes that was the moment his "switch had flipped." By now you probably know enough not to believe anything a man says once his switch is flipped, but are you listening to that small voice that's trying to lead you out of trouble? Or are you worried about being rude, mean, or perpetually single? I still don't know if the whole platonic thing was a PUA move to lower my guard and get in my pants, or if he was genuine at the beginning and I just became a convenient target of opportunity. Either way, I wish I'd trusted my gut!*

~~ A Serious Note ~~

Ladies,

I've tried to keep this book very lighthearted, but this is a serious topic, so let's just pause for a second.

As one of the founding cadet members of the U.S. Air Force Academy Cadet Sexual Assault Hotline, I take the topic of sexual assault very seriously.

All too often, victims (female AND male) are made to feel like THEY are to blame for their assault. It is not your fault! No matter what you wore, drank, said, or did up until the time you said no to unwanted sexual advances, it was NOT your fault.

Should you find yourself in this horrible situation, please consider reaching out to RAINN (Rape, Abuse & Incest

National Network), which maintains the national Sexual Assault Hotline Number: **800.656.HOPE (4673).**

Recovering from sexual assault or abuse is a process, and that process looks different for everyone. It may take weeks, months, or years; there's no timetable for healing. At www.RAINN.org, you'll find resources to help you navigate the healing process.

Date #23: Mr. Who-Is-THAT Plays the Gentleman

As I left Mr. You-Owe-Me's car, I praised God things hadn't progressed the way he wanted. Once in my apartment, I curled up on my couch.

I didn't want to be alone, but all of my girlfriends were tied up. I'd just laid down the law with Mr. Gentle-Giant, so couldn't have him over without a chaperone. And if I had a chaperone, I wouldn't need to have him over. I was afraid other guys I'd met would take advantage of my fragile state. Mr. Man came to mind, but he lived an hour away and, plus, it was too soon to have him in my house.

Out of desperation, I texted Mr. Who-Is-THAT and asked what he was up to. He was available and agreed to come watch my favorite movie with me. I felt comfortable with him, and just thinking about him being there brought me some peace.

He was quite the gentleman, staying firmly on his place on the loveseat while I curled up on the sofa. I don't remember what we talked about, but I do remember feeling safe and secure with him there in the room.

This was the first time I thought, "Maybe having a man in my life isn't such a bad idea after all!" My ex-husband would never have sat with me like that after a jarring incident. Nor would he have respected my boundaries. I began to consider that maybe, just maybe, all men weren't like my ex.

Maybe I should give them a real chance.

Moral of the Story: Be open to life lessons wherever they come! Up until this point, I was just having fun. As hurt as I was by the way he broke us up, Mr. Gap-Filler and I weren't looking for marriage. My life was much more vibrant and fulfilling after becoming single again, and I'd watched too many friends hate life after finally landing a "piece of man" to want to be bound that way myself. We were two people having a great time together. I figured it would eventually lead to marriage, but I wasn't in a rush!

When I went out with these men, it wasn't because I was wanting to get married yesterday. I wanted to prove my worth and have some fun. A free meal wouldn't hurt, either!

Several guys told me later that my "let's just take it slow and see where it goes" attitude was incredibly attractive. The men in my singles groups confirmed it. When a woman brings up marriage too soon, he doesn't feel like she cares about *him* specifically. He worries that she's just looking for the first breathing guy who can fulfill some plan driven by her biological clock.

It's a strange paradox; by not caring, if I ended up in a relationship, I was attractive to more men who wanted one. Most of these men are now married, so they, too, wanted marriage; just with a woman who truly loved and respected THEM, not just the first decent guy who came along who then changed into a stranger after marriage. That night, my outlook changed, and I took a hard look at who was actually marriage material.

Date #24: The Best Sex Response Ever!

Mr. Man was a lot of fun! He had great culinary tastes, loved sports and tonight, he was coming with me to Bible Study before dinner.

Anyone else ever feel like the one day you bring a visitor to church is the day everything goes wrong??

Poor Mr. Man! He got every "we don't like you" sermon in the book:

> "Don't you sully our precious clean, holy sister."
> "You better get right or you gonna burn in hell!"
> "Jeans in church? You think we should just be happy you showed up, don't you?!"

I was pretty sure there would be NO date #6!

During dinner, we talked about the preaching and he wanted to know where I stood on sex before marriage. This is a big deal breaker for most men, and it seems to me that, even if they would have waited, once you say you're waiting for marriage, they move on.

When I asked my singles group about this, the most common male answer was that it's not really about getting sex before marriage. It's that they don't want to end up married to a missionary-only vanilla once-a-month gal. Guys in my groups often said, "Be upfront - don't waste our time," but when I called them on the fact that they're unlikely to ask out a woman who did, most laughed and recommended something like, "I'm not in a rush. Let's just see where this goes." This says, "I'm open, but I'm not going to push you and I expect you won't push me." They enjoyed women who kept their interest while waiting with teasing and hinting at what might come, such as, "I hope we get there one day, but right now we kind of need to cool off."

Well," I ventured, "You know I'm a minister, so I'm pretty much in the 'no sex before marriage' camp."

"Ok."

"So you're ok with possibly not having sex for a couple of years?"

"What I heard was, 'One day, I might get to have sex again.' "

Moral of the Story: The right man will wait until you are comfortable with intimacy. Even if he wants more, he will understand (and respect) your decision to take things slow. We can help the process by avoiding the "dating tripwires" of talking about marriage too soon, emphatically saying no to sex before marriage and acting like we're so independent that we don't need a man for anything.

Date #25: Mr. Why-Don't-You-Drink

If you choose not to drink for religious or other reasons, I hope you'll remember that this is viewed negatively by many men and that you won't take it personal if they lose interest.

Abstaining from alcohol cost me more dates than any other facet of my personality (even more than abstaining from sex). Can you guess what answers I received when I asked men why this was? In ranked order:

1. If she doesn't drink, she doesn't put out.
2. If she doesn't drink, she's probably a recovering alcoholic (who might backslide).
3. If she doesn't drink, she is going to be a judging killjoy.

One of the best ways to weed out men who are just looking for a conquest is to not drink. Even if he'd be willing to wait for marriage, unless there's something amazing about you, he's likely to move on.

Let's face it! The majority of the adult world revolves around alcohol. Bar-hopping. Wine tastings. Brew-yoga. If you don't drink, you are automatically taking yourself out of what most people consider essential for a good time - even church folks.

When I first joined Match.com, I searched for men who didn't drink at all. In my town, there were only 32 guys who checked "don't drink" and all of them were either too old or too weird. When I changed my parameters to "social drinking," the number of available guys that met my other parameters went up to over 500. I still left MY profile as "doesn't drink," and guess what? I was contacted by guys who THEMSELVES don't drink, but changed their profile to "social drinking" because it opened up more matches for them.

However, this particular date was doomed from the start! His frustration at my ordering cranberry juice devolved into him ranting against how all women who don't drink are either religious prudes or alcoholics who are one step away from relapse!

Moral of the Story: *I'm not telling you to start drinking! I'm saying realize what signals this sends and work around it, if possible. Assure the guy that you are lots of fun and show him this by being a fun date. One way to do this is by asking him questions about himself and trying to relax.*

Date #26: Mr. Farmers-Only

This wasn't supposed to be MY date! I was actually trying to set my girlfriend up with a man I'd met on an online networking site. He was coming into town for a work conference and had free tickets to a concert.

Secular concerts aren't my thing, but my girl was in a dating slump, so I thought they would get along! My plan was to go to dinner as part of the group and then sneak away to do some shopping while they went to the concert.

Only he looked way older than I expected in person, was nowhere near as cool in person as his online personality and she wasn't diggin' his appearance. Even worse, even though I kept mentioning my friend throughout our weeks of planning leading up to the date, he thought he was on a date with ME!

It was a miserable drive back, but the discussion opened my eyes. My girlfriends were tired of me trying to set them up with guys I didn't want.

In other words, they considered those guys "sloppy seconds," and wished I would stop bringing them to our fellowships and community projects.

In my defense, I thought these were great guys who just weren't great for me because of my ministry or other extenuating factors. Mr. Farmers-Only was the only man I tried to push on my friends sight-unseen.

I'm still Facebook friends with most of these guys I tried to set my friends up with, and guess what? Most of them are married! That means they were looking to settle down, just like my friends. Mr. Cub would have been fantastic with one of my girls, as would Mr. Strong-And-Sensitive. All the single ladies in the group I ran with back then are still single.

I sure hope they'll also still be my friends after reading this paragraph, but if they're mad, I'm sorry, but it's true!

Moral of the Story: *If your friend has a strange life circumstance (like she's a minister) and she's offering you a chance to meet a former date, please don't look at it as "sloppy seconds." She may be genuinely trying to connect two great people. Two people can be amazing on their own, but not a good relationship fit for each other.*

If you're in a dating slump, and your girlfriend introduces you to a man she already went out with, please consider that perhaps she found him attractive or ideal for all but one area of her life, and that she thinks you're a good fit! At least give the guy one date! You never know where it might lead!

Date #27: Mr. Betrayal

Mr. Betrayal ran a large entertainment complex that I'd visited once or twice. He always threw in a little extra on top of that military discount, so I wasn't surprised when one day he asked me to meet him there for lunch.

I was liking Mr. Man more and more, but the way I felt about it was, "If you like me that much, you should be filling up my phone and my calendar." Mr. Man was still only visiting me once or twice a week. I didn't think about the fact that he lived an hour away. Instead, I was too focused on the fact that he was still on Match.com and there were plenty of single women in his hometown.

So I met Mr. Betrayal for lunch and, WOW, we hit it off! He'd been through a lot, had solid plans for expanding his business (a topic I can discuss all day) and we seemed to make a great team. We made plans for the next date and two days later, had a marathon eight-hour phone conversation as I was driving to an out-of-state conference.

It was then that I realized something wasn't quite right with Mr. Betrayal. He loved too hard and felt too deeply for my tastes. He'd spoken at length about how a particular woman had betrayed him by having affairs with other guys right there in his bedroom.

During that marathon phone call, I learned that he'd only dated this woman who betrayed him for about three weeks, moving her into his place after a week. And yet it had taken him eight years to get over her.

She must have been gorgeous. And/or he must have been in a very low place emotionally to put much stock in a woman he'd not even known for a month! To still be angry about it eight years later (such that it dominated our conversation) showed me he hadn't yet matured enough to deal with disappointment. And he hadn't yet taken ownership of his role in the mess.

This was adolescent behavior.

I was looking for a grown man.

Moral of the Story: *Be willing to walk away when you uncover an important deal-breaker. It may save you grief and trouble later on.*

Date #28: Mr. Gentle-Giant Doesn't Want To Take His Clothes Off

Mr. Gentle-Giant was getting tired of only seeing me at single's group and volunteer outings, and invited us to a pool party one weekend when he had visitation with his kids. Our sons were kindred spirits and loved to swim. It was a public pool, so I figured there would be others around and said, "Yes."

The kids had a great time!

I, however, was totally stressed out! You see, Mr. Gentle-Giant was incredibly good-looking and every time I was with him, I became painfully aware at how much weight I'd put on during the divorce. I felt inadequate and was sure my cellulite and stretch marks would disgust him.

Since he was already irritated at the boundaries I was putting up (due to finding out that he was technically still married), I just knew he would lose total interest once he saw my old body for what it was, and compare it to his ex (who was a gorgeous fitness instructor half my size).

I wanted so badly for him to take off his shirt and go swim, but I didn't push the issue because then I'd have to take off mine! Unlike most men who are always pressuring us to show more skin, I noticed that Mr. Gentle-Giant didn't want to swim and supported all of my excuses for staying seated when our kids begged us to play. We weren't having great conversation, so every comment he made got translated by my brain into "You're too fat and ugly."

I'm embarrassed to type this! I was good-looking and a reasonable size, but somehow fixated on comparing myself to his ex.

Finally, the boys would be denied no longer, and so I made a comment about not wanting to uncover, but having no choice. He replied that HE was nervous to take off his shirt too! He hadn't shaved in a few days and didn't like his appearance. He was just as anxious about taking off HIS shirt as I was about taking off MINE! The whole time I thought he was hating on my body, he really he was hating on HIS!

For the record, he looked amazing! That 5 o'clock body shadow accented his abs nicely and I forgot all about my cellulite and just started praying that God would hurry that divorce up so we could go out "for real" again!

Moral of the Story: *We have to watch out for old insecurities that sneak their way back into our hearts. The whole time I was stressing about his assessment of my looks, he wasn't even thinking about me! He was stressed about himself. Too often, we miss out on fun because we misinterpret someone else's issues as our own!*

Date #29: Mr. Man Wins Over My Friends

"Let's have a Lord of the Rings marathon!"

If you hear those words, RUN! Run far away and don't look back! To say I felt entrapped by each movie being over 3 hours would be an understatement. Even worse, if you didn't already understand the storyline or hadn't read the books, it was very hard to figure out what was going on.

I still shudder about this 12 hours of my life I'll never get back! I felt duped because my friends and Mr. Man were having a blast. I wondered if they'd all taken a sip of something before I got there because I just didn't get it!

The day was not all lost, though. Mr. Man and I snuggled on the loveseat.

After about 10 hours, people's true personalities began to come out and Mr. Man retained his chill, laid back, behavior. After he left, I had a heart to heart with my friends. What did they think of him?

My friends decided Mr. Man was a perfect match for me. "This is the kind of guy you SHOULD be dating!" they told me. "Not the jerks you keep bringing home or talking about like Mr. Gap-Filler!"

Apparently, they were tired of me complaining about my various dates and all the many ways Mr. Gap-Filler did me wrong. They liked Mr. Man, and felt he fit in nicely with our little group of friends.

Moral of the Story: *Your friends love you. They want the best for you! Let them speak into the relationship arena of your life!*

Date #30: Mr. Inconsistently-Athletic

Did you know that if you list yourself in the wrong body category (too big or too small), you might struggle to find a man who loves you the way you are? A person can be thin, but still be out of shape, so the first time I dated online, I listed myself as "athletic," which I now know is online dating code for "thin," about size 0-6ish. Sizes 8-14 was considered average/normal, 16-18 "a few extra pounds," and if you list yourself as "curvy," most online daters will expect you to be size 20+.

I was pretty hurt that men thought I'd lied about my appearance. I am VERY athletic. I can deadlift 240 lbs. I'm muscular and have a great hourglass shape. I attracted many men interested in fitness who were angry (and sometimes disgusted) when they saw that my hourglass figure really was an HOURglass and not a MINUTEglass.

This time around, I knew better and selected average, but Mr. Inconsistently-Athletic slipped through the cracks. He, himself, was the epitome of health. A busy executive, he still made time for fitness and it showed. We went out a few times and I'd even stopped by his apartment once. If a man made it to a fourth date, I offered to cook dinner (after all, he'd already paid for three by then) and that's when the criticism began. Pointing out items in my pantry, he began to lecture. If I would "just" stop eating this, start doing that, I could look fantastic!

First of all, I already looked fantastic! Second of all, I'd seen his fridge and what he was feeding his children: Mystery-meat hotdogs with white bread and processed cheese food. Not even real cheese. Cheese food. You know the stuff: mostly oil, not milk. So clearly, he wasn't concerned for my overall health.

Moral of the Story: *His real problem was that my appearance didn't meet his idea of what made HIM look good to other men. He liked everything else about me and had hoped he could work with me to fit the role of "hot woman on his arm." He wasn't concerned about what his kids ate because their status was more a reflection on his ex-wife than on him. It's not a sin for a man to want his wife to look good. Most do, even if they won't tell you. It boosts their ego and helps them feel satisfied that they made the right decision to commit to you when you look fabulous next to them.*

After our first date, you knew what I looked like. If it was a problem, there shouldn't have been a 2nd date. One thing I've learned about men who are always trying to fix me: there's always a problem. You fix one, and now it's something else. They are never satisfied. In my first marriage, my self esteem took a huge hit because of this, and I wasn't going down THAT road again! Ain't nobody got time for that! Not this lady right heyah!

Date #31: Mr. Man Shows Me Off

One way you know a relationship is moving forward is when a man invites you to meet the important people in his life: coworkers, friends, family, etc.

When I was younger, I took great umbrage with the concept of men "showing off his woman." I'm not some piece of property designed to boost your ego! I had the same ire when men would hold the door open (I can get it myself) or offer to lift my carryon bag to the overhead bin (I've got it, thanks). Men who complimented me would be met with a scowl (who do you think you are).

I've come to realize that allowing men to help me helps me get far more done than insisting I don't need them. Rewarding compliments with "thank you" and a smile makes his day and usually pays off later when I realize I need help or end up working with him.

So while I was a bit creeped out that everyone at Mr. Man's school knew who I was and was excited to meet me, at the same time, it was reassuring! It meant he was taken with me, and everyone knew it. I came away from that first football game confident that he was really into me.

Being strong, independent women, we sometimes overlook the power in having a man that wants to show us off. After all, we're not just a piece of meat! Unless he has self-image problems, showing you off is a good sign that he's truly happy to be with you! Let him!

I have a similar conversation with ladies from my Christian singles group when it comes to sex.

"Why do they keep pressuring me for sex when I've said I'm waiting for marriage?"

My response always surprises them: "Why do you want them to stop wanting you?"

Look, you've been keeping yourself all these years, right? Once that ring goes on your finger, you have to make up for lost time! You WANT a man who can't keep his hands off you.

My husband and I dated for two and a half years, and he NEVER stopped trying. He's the red-blooded, gun-totin,' excels-at-his-job man I'd been praying for, and that kind of man wants a woman who will be worth the wait!

I found out later that even if I HAD acquiesced, he would have backed off for fear of God. That still didn't stop him from trying, though!

Moral of the Story: *Don't kick your man to the curb if he shows you off or just because you have to send him home hot and bothered after every date. Be happy he's hot for you. It's a blessing! Look! Too many women are trapped in marriages with a man who thinks they're too fat, too ugly, too whatever and tells them so constantly. Enjoy the fact that he's turned on by you; it means you are attractive and that he values you!*

Date #32: Mr. I'm-Not-Intimidated

This good-looking Army ranger showed promise. He was shorter, but broad-shouldered, just the way I liked 'em.

We had light, easy conversation over a delectable dinner until he asked what I do.

"I'm in the military," I told him.

"Yeah, but what do you DO?"

"Admin work." This is the same answer I gave everyone because I learned early in when you tell guys you are a physicist, their eyes glaze over and they lose interest.

"What kind of admin work?"

"You know, taskers and stuff."

"Seriously, what is your MOS? Why don't you want to tell me what you do?"

For those who don't know, MOS is Army parlance for "Military Occupational Specialty" code, which is a way of describing your career field.

"Fine. I'm a physicist in the Air Force."

** Eyes glaze over. Crickets chirping. **

"Really? Wow! Why didn't you want to tell me? You probably thought I'd be intimidated ...Well, I'm not."

I heard that same sentence about six times throughout dinner and three more times when he called later for a 2nd date. He never got one.

Moral of the Story: *When a woman's education or earning power is higher than that of her date, he may pre-judge that he isn't good enough or can't make her happy. Today's high-earning woman tends to attract those looking for a sugar momma and push away the kind of guy she typically wants. Be aware of this dynamic and strive to be the woman your ideal man is looking for. This doesn't mean change who you are. While I haven't changed who I am for Mr. Man, I'm always looking for ways he can help me.*

One time, my husband and I were living in separate states. I had a lot of stuff to load and left it for him because he was coming to visit. One of my single coworkers laughed at me. "I can move my own boxes," she said. "Yes you can," I replied, "and so can I, but he loves to feel needed." I might ask him to open a can, or reach an item high on the shelf even though I can easily grab the stepstool. It makes him feel like a "man" and independent women who want an alpha male must look for ways to give him that pleasure.

Date #33: Mr. Man Messes Up

Mr. Man and I were now spending about 2-3 evenings a week together and I felt like we were heading in a great direction. I wasn't sure how I'd handle my upcoming military deployment and move (I hadn't told him yet), but I figured the Lord would work that out. For all of my teaching singles about how "You're never exclusive until the man says so," or, "It's not official until it's Facebook official," I found myself focusing only on him.

Again, I've always felt that if a man wanted me to be his alone, he needs to fill up so much of my schedule that there's no room for any other man to slip in. That's easy to say... yet I wasn't even following my own rules! I was beginning to feel like we were "a thing."

His students and coworkers knew me. He had assimilated fairly well into my group of friends. After one of the many football games I attended to watch him work, one of his students, Chyna, asked if I was his girlfriend. I looked at him beaming, excited to hear him say what I'd been feeling in my heart.

"No, but we're headed that way."

The world stopped, and I felt like I'd been gut punched!! How on earth had I been played like that?

I smiled nicely and got through the rest of the event without embarrassing myself or him. When I got home, the first thing I did was open up Match.com and respond back to every man who'd contacted me in the last week or so. I'll tell you about those dates soon.

The next day, Mr. Man came to hang out and the air was tense. I tried hard not to be angry at him, feeling like it was

MY fault for letting my guard down when he still hadn't initiated "the talk."

I'm in the bathroom responding to a guy on Match.com, when I notice he's also online and had some new activity on his profile. REALLY??? You're at MY house trolling Match?? Nah, Boo! I'm'a need you to do better!

Let's set aside the fact that I was on there at the same time. Let's also set aside the fact that I may or may not have quickly created a fake profile to entrap him while in that bathroom. And since we're setting things aside, let's just ignore that 10 days ago, I'd gone out with Mr. "I'm-Not-Intimidated." Right or wrong, I was angry!

Feeling disrespected, I sent the man home.

Moral of the Story: *We have to know what we want in a relationship and have enough confidence and self-respect to walk away if our needs aren't being met. I'm not talking about being unreasonable and expecting a man to cater to our every whim. I still wanted to see him, but I wasn't about to sit at home alone if he was seeking other women the other five days of the week we weren't together.*

Date #34: Mr. Booty-Call

The first person I went out with while thinking Mr. Man was playing me was a thin, wiry fellow who kept insisting he was 35 years old and too mature to play games.

> If someone has to tell you they don't play games, they probably do.
>
> If volunteers that they don't hit women, they probably do.
>
> Or that they don't do drugs/prostitutes/etc., they probably do.

Your average dater doesn't feel the need to say these things during a first or second date unless it comes up in conversation. There's a difference between saying, "I don't understand why some men think it's ok to hit women" when you were just talking about the weather, and saying it after watching a viral video about someone who overcame domestic violence.

I was tired of Mr. Booty Call's conversation before we'd even ordered dinner. Just finding a restaurant was quite the ordeal. The venue I had selected (a low-key Thai place) was closed on Monday nights. We couldn't figure out where to go. He kept insisting that he didn't know the area very well and wanted me to pick something. I finally picked a nearby Japanese place, but the whole exchange was unfulfilling.

Remember, I was no longer just dating to have fun and prove I was desirable (I'd already proven that to myself, whether or not Mr. Gap-Filler ever discovered it). I was now looking for a partner. And I don't need a partner who plans to take me out and doesn't at least look up what's in the nearby location. Sorry, guys! I spend all day "being a man" at work. I shouldn't have to be one in the evening, too.

The restaurant was packed and kindly requested we depart. We walked to a nearby park to talk some more. He asked if I'd come to his apartment, which was right around the corner! What? He lives here? Why all that, "You choose: I don't know this area?"

You're probably laughing at just how long it took me to figure out he only wanted that booty! I went out with so many great guys you've read about, so I just wasn't expecting it.

Moral of the Story: *Some guys really are just after one thing. Don't internalize that! It has nothing to do with you. If I hadn't gone out with so many great guys, I might have thought "This is the only kind of man out there." Not so! Keep looking and you'll find the one who complements you perfectly!*

Date #35: Mr. Won't-Marry-His-Live-In

Being military, I've moved a lot. One day, a handsome coworker from a previous base reached out to me on Facebook. He, too, was now divorced and remembered that we got along well back in the day. He was moving to my new base and wanted to meet for lunch.

YES! I knew this guy to be one of the "good guys" who didn't cheat on his wife when our team worked out of town on military trips. My excitement quickly faded, though, as the date grew nearer and I began to dig into his Facebook page.

His girlfriend from another state moved down here with him! They lived in a rent home together with all of their kids and there were pictures of her plastered (mostly of her tagging) all over his page.

I almost cancelled the lunch, but then decided it would be fun to make him uncomfortable. After all, he'd almost put me in the awkward position of being "the other woman."

After a good bit of chit-chat, I came out and asked him about so-and-so, letting him know I saw that she had moved down with him, and that I wondered if they'd broken up suddenly. His response floored me!

"Oh, well that's just temporary!"

"Does she know that?"

"Of course she does! If she really wanted marriage, she would have required that before moving in with me. We both know it's going nowhere. It's just convenient."

"Um… I think most women view moving in together as a step toward marriage."

He disagreed, vehemently, and I decided to ask every single man I knew who had a live-in girlfriend. Do you know that in three years of asking, only ONE man I spoke with had any intention of marrying his live-in girlfriend? He was deploying to Afghanistan after checking into a new base. He brought her with him, bought the house for her to live in and then went off to war. They married when he returned. He's literally the only one! All of the other men said the exact same thing to me: "Of course we're not going to get married! If she wanted that, she shouldn't have moved in without at least an engagement ring on her finger."

Moral of the Story: I had to learn to stop judging men based on chick-flicks and what *I* wanted. I had to learn how men think and what really turns them on. I had to learn that men value what they strive for, not what's just handed to them. Too many of the men I spoke with viewed their live-in girlfriend as more a convenient caretaker and sexpot than someone they wanted to spend the rest of their life with. Please be wary of that!

Date #36: Mr. Beef-Cake's Free Therapy

I'd drooled over Mr. Beef-Cake for about a year, but he never thought to ask me out until he found that I was dating online.

He was tall, broad and hairy like Mr. Man. I still tend towards shorter, barrel-chested men, but these tall guys were growing on me.

We hit it off and both had very compatible ministries. He, too, was a military parent, and quickly volunteered to mentor any men who found their way to my non-profit Military Single Moms (and Dads).

We were both were looking for sweet, kind people versus the party guy/gal everyone else seemed to be looking for. We also both had artistic sides - something few of my dates possessed.

The only blemish in what could have been a lovely romance was that he was really into beer. As a tee totaling minister, I noted this but figured if it was meant to be, the Lord would work it out!

After six hours, it was time to go home. He gave me a big hug instead of a kiss. I was disappointed, but figured we'd fix that next time. Only he didn't ask for a next time! Instead, he told me one day he hoped I could meet this friend he was thinking of dating.

His WHAT???

She was really sweet, but he wasn't sure about being tied down again and, apparently, my opinions helped confirm for him that she's just the kind of lady he should be with. He said I encouraged him by saying he deserved someone sweet who would appreciate him and take care of him. She was, and he thought I would approve of her!

I maintained my dignity and expressed how happy I was for him.

In my mind, we had a future!

In his mind, he was just hanging out with a cool girl!

They married about a year later and are very happy.

Moral of the Story: *I firmly believe all of these dates weren't just so I could have a good time. Sure, some were! Others were ordained to build the men up, and still others were ordained to build me up or teach me valuable life lessons. Most of the men I dated ended up in happy marriages, and I am thankful for this "summer of love" that taught me so much about men and relationships.*

Date #37: Mr. Who-Is-THAT and Why "So Much Chemistry" is a Lie

Mr. Man had most of the traits I wanted in a mate, including something most men don't do anymore: standing up for their woman. Few dates stood up for me when servers laughed at me for not drinking. It happens more than you would imagine, and most dates laughed it off or joined in the teasing. Not cool!

You might remember Mr. Club-Owner as one of two men who came to church with me. I would visit him after Friday Night Light (church service) at about the same time he was closing down his venues. He was the first man in my life who would take up for me when one of his performers had something to say about Jesus or religious girls, or the fact that I didn't drink. He was good to me and met a need I didn't even know I had because it had gone unmet all of my life!

And Mr. Man was the same way! It was one of the first things I loved about him!

My problem was that Mr. Man is not the type to talk about deep, philosophical concepts. Oh, he liked to talk! He could replay every TV show he ever watched and quote an amazing amount of trivia. He just didn't have much appetite for in-depth discourse on how we're going to change the world. I felt powerful chemistry with Mr. Who-Is-THAT and men like him because of the intense conversation we shared.

One day, Mr. Who-Is-THAT and I walked through a popular outdoor mall, deep in conversation when it hit me. I am not compatible with this man! He's just like the men from my prayer last night.

You see, the Spirit revealed to me that I would never find love if I kept chasing after chemistry. Why? The kind of guy

I always had strong chemistry with would never marry a woman like me!

He was gregarious, driven, well-spoken and well-traveled. This type of man couldn't tell you why he didn't have solid long-term relationships. He just didn't. As one explained it: "I was really into her, and then I just wasn't! Nothing she did wrong." This man enjoyed academic discourse with a beautiful, quality woman, but would never marry someone as accomplished and confident as me whose willingness to call him out and be direct fed into his inner demons.

Moral of the Story: *Chemistry doesn't mean compatibility! In fact, the authors of **Reinvent Your Life** say that usually intense chemistry leads us to choose mates that will hurt us. He is still one of the most amazing guys I've ever known! I had to learn to stop trying to make it work when it was clear he was not a good fit for me and where I was going with my life.*

Date #38: Mr. Happy-Birthday

Once I had the chemistry revelation, my prospects for a long-term relationship dropped drastically. I was ok with that, trusting that I was onto something that would break the cycle of abusive and demeaning relationships I'd had in the past.

Mr. Man and I may not have had conversational chemistry, and I was still pretty cool to him after the "not my girlfriend" incident, but when we were together, we couldn't keep our hands off each other! I loved the fact that he found my idiosyncrasies adorable, rather than annoying, and we just made such a good team!

There's only one man who truly challenged Mr. Man's #1 spot in my heart. Mr. Happy-Birthday and I had instant chemistry! We connected so thoroughly that in just days of meeting each other, it looked like we were old friends. When we went shopping together, store owners who saw us thought we'd been partners-in-crime, happily married 20 years and having the adventure of a lifetime. I had plenty of time to talk to these shop-owners because HE out shopped ME! I loved it!

He combined all the manly traits I admired, such as using firearms to keep his family safe along with the suave good looks and modern style I desired to be seen with. Yeah, you can call me vain! I don't believe women should plan on changing a man, but I was going to have to do something about Mr. Man's old guy wardrobe if we had a future!

Mr. Happy-Birthday loved to travel, was well-spoken and pursuing his PhD in a very competitive field. He had successfully navigated the dangerous waters of growing up a "Black in America" and I was confident he could guide my son into becoming a man. I was impressed!

The best part about it was that even though I was the heaviest I'd ever been in my life, he seemed to think I was gorgeous! Who can resist a man who thinks she isn't just "fine," but, "fo-iiii-nnne."

I had to be realistic about things, though. I knew I was called to the ministry and would one day be a pastor. His worldview was just not compatible with mine, and no amount of mutual respect and strong physical connection was going to help us weather the eventual storms that come from being a pastor's husband.

Moral of the Story: *A good marriage is built just as much on partnership and compatibility as it is chemistry. Resist the urge to hold on to someone who's not a good "lifestyle and calling" fit just because of chemistry or looks.*

Date #39: Mr. Man Explains

Mr. Man felt the rub of my going out with other guys. We were only seeing each other once a week because my calendar was full. Finally, he asked if he'd done something wrong. I explained that he had done nothing wrong, but since we weren't moving in the direction I wanted, I was exploring other options.

"What are you talking about?" he asked in frustration.

"You were sitting on my couch emailing women on Match.com. You told Chyna I wasn't your girlfriend, but we were headed that way."

"That's what this is about?" He threw up his hands and continued. "I was on Match telling women I was no longer available. And Chyna didn't ask if you were my girlfriend! She asked if you were my FIANCÉ!"

Don't you hate when someone takes the wind out of your sails in the middle of an argument where you just knew you were right??

I still don't know if I heard Chyna wrong (I doubt it), or if he was just back-peddling. I do remember that he didn't tell my fake Match profile he was seeing someone else, so while I made peace for the night, I wasn't 100% satisfied with his explanation. After all, no matter the reason, it's incredibly poor form to be on a dating website while your date is in the bathroom.

When you've met the love of your life, I would expect you to close down your profile or hide it temporarily so no one else can contact you for a while. He did neither. It might have been a genuine mistake. I found out later I was only the second woman he'd dated since becoming single again, so perhaps he wanted to know that he's "still got it." Maybe he wasn't sold on me yet and was playing the field.

I'll never know because I'm not going to ask. What I do know is that conversation ended with us deciding to be exclusive, close down our Match.com profiles and stop going out with others. In all transparency, I kept my profile for two more weeks before I closed it… just to make sure HE wasn't still active! Also, my being willing to draw a line made him respect me more.

Moral of the Story: *If you are highly emotive, like I am, it's easy to spiral into the depths of despair over a misunderstanding, or float on cloud nine over something minor that others wouldn't even notice. We have to temper our feelings long enough to talk about what bothers us and get more details before taking strong action that we'll regret later! We waste too much of our time and energy reacting to things that never even happened.*

Date #40: Mr. Man Seals The Deal

That night, we dressed up and went to one of my favorite steakhouses to celebrate our new status. We made it "Facebook official" and had two more fun-filled months before I deployed.

My good-bye speech was crafted from the reality of other women who were devastated when their long-distance sweethearts had local honeys to take her place. "It's been fun, but I know long-distance doesn't really work, so if I don't hear from you again, it's ok. I understand."

He called or Skyped me every night for over two years, including while I was in the Middle East. He came to visit me a couple of times at my new duty location, and by time he proposed, I was sure, despite the distance, that he was the one!

Moral of the Story: I hope every single lady reading these words who desires to be in a relationship finds the love she is looking for! May you meet a wonderful man who loves you just the way you are, whose skillset complements yours and who makes living life easier and more exciting!

Epilogue

I hope you've had fun reading about my dating adventures, *40 Dates in 4 Months*! I learned a LOT about men and dating during that time, and I tried to incorporate the most important lessons into this book.

Please reach out to me to let me know what you liked best and how this book has helped you. If you choose to date, I'd love to hear if you've been able to apply any of these lessons from it to your love life.

Blessings,

Janine "JJ" Conway
2008 Airline Dr #300-159
Bossier City, LA 71111

Your Turn!

Would you like to be a part of the next collection of our dating stories?

We are collecting stories from those who have been inspired by this book. They will be compiled into a 2nd edition that will, like this, be sold as a fundraiser for our singles ministry.

Please reach out to me to submit your chapter, or to just tell me how it's going!

Blessings,

Janine "JJ" Conway
2008 Airline Dr #300-159
Bossier City, LA 71111

Author Bio:

Janine "JJ" Conway has been involved in financial ministry for over 20 years. She is humbled to serve as Founder and CEO of Hand-Ups Not Hand-Outs, LLC, whose mission is to empower your dreams through financial and real estate education, advanced financial planning techniques and leadership development. She loves helping people dump debt, build wealth and leave a legacy!

Growing up overseas, she developed a zeal for adventure and deep appreciation for the blessings of being American. She has a BS in Physics from the U.S. Air Force Academy and an MS in Nuclear Engineering from the AF Institute of Technology. JJ obtained her financial planning certificate from George Mason University and her compassion from "The School of Hard Knocks."

JJ's talks and books on church administration, personal growth and wealth building are uplifting. Uplevel your next event with one of JJ's keynotes, seminars, or full-day workshops. Booking info at www.JJConway.org.

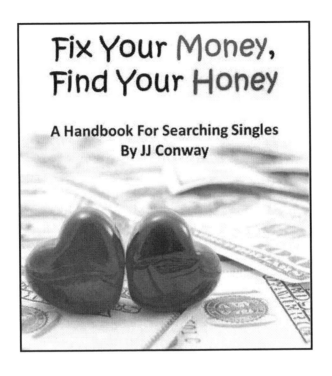

Fix Your Money,
Find Your Honey

A Handbook For Searching Singles
By JJ Conway

Bring JJ's Most Popular Singles Workshop to
YOUR
Church!
Campus!
Singles Group!

For more information visit:

www.JJConway.org

Made in the USA
Columbia, SC
24 April 2019